ABNORMAL FIELD GUIDES TO CRYPTIC CREATURES

THE
BUNYIP

WORLD
BOOK

www.worldbook.com

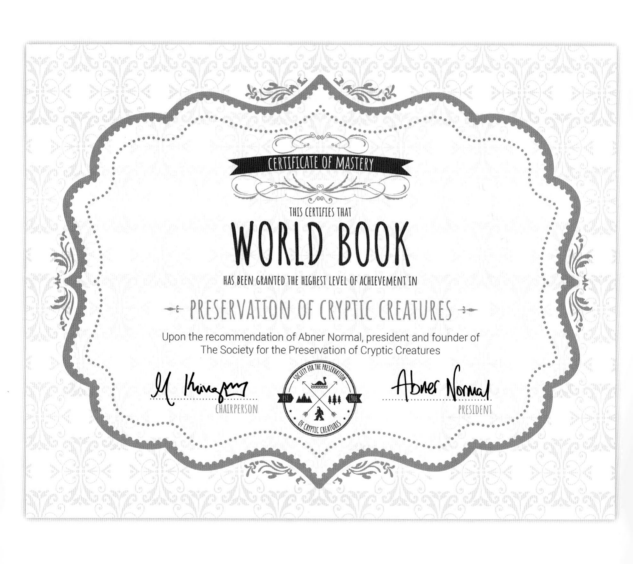

Contents

How to use this book

A field guide is a book written to help you identify and learn about animals or other things in nature. The "field" part is just a fancy way of saying you're supposed to carry the book with you while tramping about in the wild. A normal field guide will fit in your pocket. This one very probably will not.

A normal field guide is also filled with normal sorts of information about wombats and willow trees provided by normal experts. This field guide deals with the Bunyip, a legendary monster said to haunt watery areas of the Australian wilderness. Bunyip "experts" tend to be a mixed bag of storytellers, tricksters, and outright leg-pullers. You'll just have to deal with it.

The following items may be useful in your search for the Bunyip:

Camera

Drinking water

Earplugs
(The Bunyip is known to howl.)

Sturdy boots

Tent

Caution:

If you have ever listened to a spooky story, you know that it is dangerous to head off into the wilderness in search of legendary monsters. So wear comfortable shoes, and be sure to ask a parent's permission.

What's that name?

For the uninformed, the name Bunyip may conjure images of a jolly creature who brings people cinnamon buns, or hot cross buns, or even hamburger buns for their summer cookout. But those people are wrong. The Bunyip would most likely eat all those things—and you.

The name Bunyip is sometimes said to mean *devil* or *demonic spirit* in the language of Australia's Aboriginal people, the first people of Australia. The Bunyip has a fearsome reputation for attacking the unwary.

Appearance

This is where it starts to get tricky. Normal field guides include detailed descriptions of various creatures, so that you can identify them on sight. But, in the case of the Bunyip, there isn't one clear description.

People have described the Bunyip in all sorts of weird and scary ways. In their spookiest voices, they have described it as looking like a dog, a duck, an alligator, a seal, or a bird. Others have described it as a manlike or snakelike creature with the head of a horse or emu; with big teeth; with really sharp claws; and with webbed hands, fur, and glowing red eyes. But, they all agree on one thing: the Bunyip is downright creepy.

Stay away from the water!

According to legend, the Bunyip creeps in or near watery areas, but not fun water places like water parks. The Bunyip lives in *billabongs* (water holes), lakes, creeks, swamps, and rivers. So, we can't pinkie promise, but water parks are probably safe.

Sound

The Bunyip cries a terrible, terrible sound. It's like a combination of a fussy baby, a roaring lion, and the scratching of nails on a chalkboard. It howls its deepest, scariest howl so that people miles or kilometers away can feel it tingle up their spines. Noise-cancelling headphones won't help.

Range

Sightings of the Bunyip have been reported in mainland Australia and in Tasmania, an island off the continent's southeastern corner. You may have heard of another Tasmanian, the Tasmanian devil. Like the Bunyip, the Tasmanian devil screeches a terrible screech.

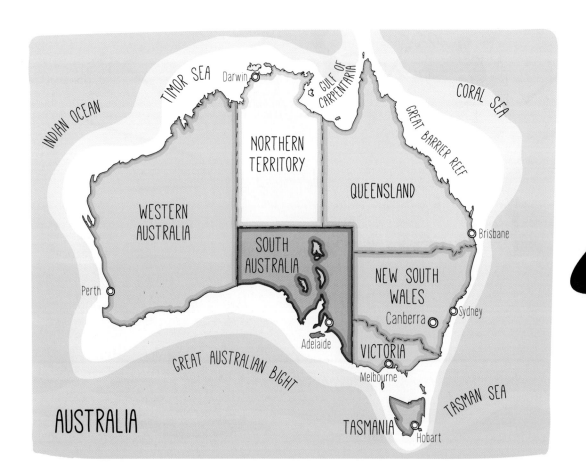

Dreamtime

Modern tales of the Bunyip may have their origins in Dreamtime. Dreamtime is a fundamental spiritual concept that connects traditional beliefs and practices among the Aboriginal people of Australia. Two parts make up Dreamtime. The first is ancient time. The second is a sacred world in which the first beings and other creatures exist. This includes such monsters as the Bunyip.

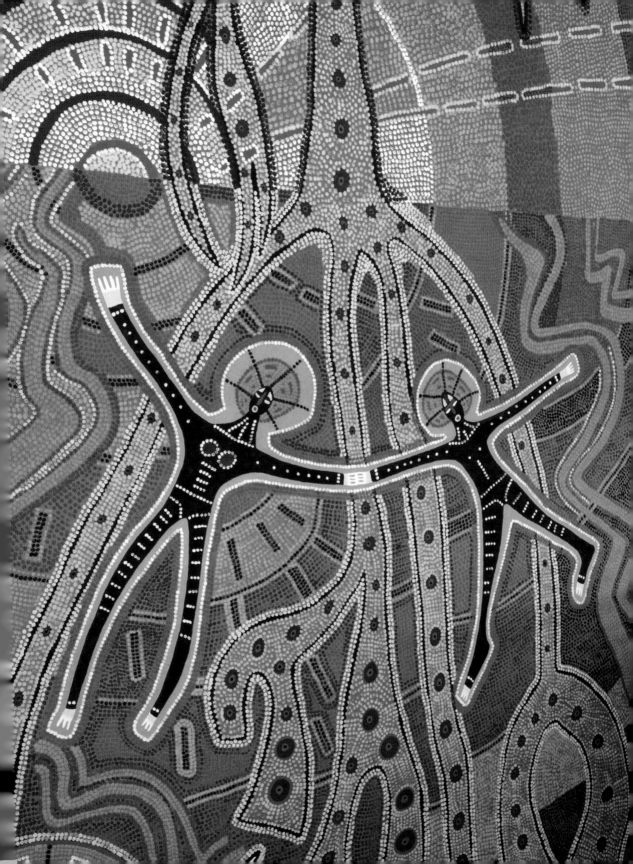

Scared settlers

You know who was even more scared of the Bunyip than small children? Australia's early European settlers. Settlers began arriving on the continent in the late 1700's, and it didn't take long for tales of the Bunyip to reach their ears. Some feared the monster so much that they thought *any* and *every* creature they hadn't seen before was the Bunyip. Some people think that Aboriginal Australians used tales of the Bunyip to spook the new arrivals.

It seems to have worked.

Habitat

Before setting off in search of the Bunyip, it may be helpful to familiarize yourself with various aspects of the creature's habitat.

THE OUTBACK

is a huge wilderness area covering as much 80 percent of Australia's interior. The Outback is a region with huge deserts, few people, and all sorts of wild creatures—the perfect place for the Bunyip to hide.

BILLABONGS.

The Bunyip likes to live in water, and *billabongs* provide a likely spot. A billabong is a small pool or lake, often one that is created by seasonal rains or floods and dries up when the weather changes.

Habitat

(continued)

CATTLE AND SHEEP.

Since the 1800's, vast areas of the Outback have been used to graze cattle and sheep. These could provide food for the Bunyip, though the creature is said to prefer people.

The platypus.

The Bunyip may sound like it has an odd mix of features, but it's got nothing on another Australian, the platypus. This strange mammal has a bill like a duck, fur like a beaver, and webbed feet like any number of creatures.

Bunyip sightings

People have reported sightings of the Bunyip since the 1800's. That's even before your grandparents were born. Some Bunyip investigators consider the creature to be a *cryptid*, a living thing whose existence has been suggested but not confirmed. Also, "Bunyip investigator" sounds like an awesome job— though definitely scary.

Bunyip Investigator »

Commonly mistaken for the Bunyip

Just because something is scary doesn't mean that it's the Bunyip. Here, for comparison, are several creatures that the uninformed might mistake for the Bunyip.

POOKA, OR PÚCA.

This phantom fairy creature is from Celtic folklore and Irish fairy tales. Like the Bunyip, Pooka can take many forms: a horse, bull, or young woman, to name a few. Settlers' memories of the Pooka may have informed their ideas about the Bunyip.

SEAL.

A few species of seal can be found in Australia's coastal waters, and some descriptions of the Bunyip sound a lot like seals.

Commonly mistaken for the Bunyip

(continued)

KANGAROO.

These marsupials are native to Australia. It's possible that some people have mistaken these animals for the Bunyip. Perhaps they thought the joey in a mama's pouch was a child being devoured. Common mistake.

STARFISH.

Some people have reported that the Bunyip looks like a gigantic starfish. There are about 1,500 species of starfish. Some of them have as many as 40 arms, or more—the better to trap you with!

Evidence

People have found strange skulls, bones, and fossils—proof that the Bunyip exists! Except . . . not exactly. Sometimes, the bones were fossilized remains of prehistoric animals. In 1846, the Australian Museum of Sydney was sure it had a Bunyip skull. But the skull belonged to a deformed horse. Well, some people did say the Bunyip had the face of a horse.

THE BUNYIP

Warning to children

By telling kids to look out for the Bunyip, adults may have hoped to scare children from going by themselves to the water's edge, where they risk drowning. So, scary tales of the Bunyip are also practical—they help keep kids safe.

Don't play water sports with the Bunyip.

The Bunyip is used to treading water. But it wouldn't win your game of water polo by scoring points. Instead, it would probably just gobble you up. And then it would keep on splashing—the Bunyip does not follow the common advice to wait 30 minutes to swim after eating.

Bunyip dos and don'ts

(continued)

DO BRING THE BUNYIP A BOX OF DISGUISES.

The Bunyip must get tired of shapeshifting into endless combinations of a variety of animals. It might need a new outfit. How about that ugly sweater your aunt gave you?

Don't call someone a bunyip.

Tales of the Bunyip are wild and exaggerated. As a result, people have used the word *bunyip* to label something or someone as a fake or impostor.

Fellow Australians

The Bunyip isn't the only mysterious creature said to lurk Down Under.

DROP BEARS.

Tales are spread of a *carnivorous* (meat-eating) koala that likes to drop from the branches of eucalyptus trees, preying on unsuspecting tourists. Not to worry, this one's definitely a *hoax* (deliberate prank). Koalas are vegetarians, dining almost exclusively on eucalyptus.

YOWIE

is a humanlike creature said to live in Australia's coastal and forest areas. Yowie is also called "Joogabina," "Gubba," "Yahoo," and "Quinkin." It is described as a large, hairy ape that walks on two legs, somewhat like Bigfoot of North America.

Celebrity status

The Bunyip is an Australian celebrity, depicted in books, films, and other artistic works. There's even a town named Bunyip in the Australian state of Victoria, which also has a Bunyip River. A weekly newspaper called *The Bunyip* serves the town of Gawler in South Australia.

Classification

With a variety of descriptions and lack of solid evidence, it's difficult to guess how the Bunyip might be related to other creatures. Some scholars think Aboriginal tales of the Bunyip may have been inspired by fossils or prehistoric encounters with beasts that are now extinct.

THE MIHIRUNG,

also called the thunderbird, was a flightless bird nearly 10 feet (3 meters) tall that weighed more than 1,000 pounds (450 kilograms). Remember that some descriptions of the Bunyip give it the head of an emu, another flightless bird.

THE GIANT WOMBAT,

also known as *Diprotodon,* was the largest marsupial that ever lived. *Diprotodon* reached up to 12 ½ feet (3.8 meters) in length and weighed nearly 6,600 pounds (3,000 kilograms), about the size of a rhinoceros. Crikey!

Many scientists doubt that the Bunyip exists. They think that reports of strange noises or sightings are often just different Australian creatures in the wilderness. Perhaps a pack of dogs, ducks, alligators, walruses, and horses were having a pool party and yelping because they were having so much fun. (Though that is unlikely.)

Some people think there will never be any physical evidence of the Bunyip's existence, because it is a sacred, otherworldly creature of the Dreamtime.

Index

WRITTEN BY MADELINE KING
ILLUSTRATIONS BY JULIAN BAKER, FAMILYTREE

Directed by Tom Evans
Edited by Jeff De La Rosa
Designed by Matt Carrington
Photo edited by Rosalia Bledsoe
Proofread by Nathalie Strassheim
Indexed by David Pofelski
Manufacturing led by Anne Fritzinger

World Book, Inc.
180 North LaSalle Street, Suite 900
Chicago, Illinois 60601
USA

For information about other World Book print and digital publications, please go to

www.worldbook.com or call 1-800-WORLDBK (967-5325).

For information about sales to schools and libraries,
call 1-800-975-3250 (United States) or 1-800-837-5365 (Canada).

Library of Congress Cataloging-in-Publication Data for this volume has been applied for.

Abnormal Field Guides to Cryptic Creatures
ISBN: 978-0-7166-4149-0 (set, hc.)

The Bunyip
ISBN: 978-0-7166-4151-3 (hc.)

Also available as:
ISBN: 978-0-7166-4159-9 (e-book)

Printed in the United States of America
by CG Book Printers, North Mankato, Minnesota
1st printing March 2020

© Alamy Images: 17 (Craft Alan King); © Bridgeman Images: 8 (Look and Learn);
© Dreamstime: 38 (Guybrushlives); © Shutterstock: 5, 14, 15, 20-23, 25, 34-37, 45;
State Library of Victoria: 9; © Tachyphylaxis: 40-41; © Warner Bros.: 14-15.

WORLD BOOK
www.worldbook.com